I Confess

Maggie Rose teaches at Milan University. She has run playwriting and theatre translation workshops throughout Europe. Her stage plays, *Six Months Here, Six Months There* (co-written with Emanuella Rossini) and *Scars of War* (co-written with Wilma G. Stark and Carlo Iacucci) explore themes of immigration, while *You in Me: Me in You* (co-written with Carla Sanguineti) puts Mary Shelley centre stage. She translated and co-adapted Renato Gabrielli's *Mobile Thriller*, dubbed the smallest show on the 2004 Edinburgh Fringe. In 2006 she co-translated Bond's *The War Plays* with Salvatore Cabras at the Winter Olympics Arts Festival in Turin.

Andy Arnold is founder and Artistic Director of the Arches – both the arts centre and its in house theatre company. He established the Arches in 1991 and it is now one of Europe's leading cultural houses. He has devised and directed the majority of in house work – most recently Dante's *Inferno*, *Spend A Penny, Beowulf*, and currently the world premiere of a James Kelman play, *Herbal Remedies*. Prior to the Arches he has been Director of the Bloomsbury Theatre, London, and Artistic Director of Theatre Workshop, Edinburgh.

fairpla

I Confess

Monologues edited by Maggie Rose

Lynsey Murdoch Alexander Hutchison **Tom Murray** Stewart Ennis **Skye Loneragan** Iain Heggie **Eliza Shackleton** Mahmood Farzan **Pauline Goldsmith** Mary Wells **Andrew Dallmeyer** Wilma G. Stark **Martin O'Connor** Alicia Devine.

fairplay press

First published by fairplay press, an imprint of Capercaillir Books Limited in 2008

Registered office 1 Rutland Court, Edinburgh.

© Capercaillie Books Limited.

The moral rights of the authors have been asserted.

Printed in the UK.

A catalogue record for this book is available from the British Library.

ISBN 978-1-906220-23-5

ARCHES

Playwrights'
Studio,
Scotland

Contents

Introduction

Many years ago I visited a tiny basement theatre in Milan to see a contemporary reworking of *Miss Julie*. As the start of this one-woman play drew near, I realised, with embarrassment, that I was the only spectator. I felt the responsibility of an entire audience on my shoulders and there was no escaping. This was my first experience of one to one theatre and it was gripping. More recently I came across Walter Manfre's work. For some time this Italian director has been experimenting with what he calls 'teatro dell'individuo' ('theatre of the individual'). *Il Viaggio* (*The Journey*) is set in a train and *La Confessione* (*Confession*) takes place in a Catholic church, complete with priests and confessionals. The first divides the audience into groups of four who in the intimate space of a six-seater compartment are invited to watch a couple of actors performing a short play, after which they move into another compartment for another play and then on again. The second consists in a number of five minute monologues, performed on a one-to-one basis, involving a priest (an audience member) and a character (an actor) who confesses his or her sins.

In a bid to explore further the potential of this theatre in miniature, I decided to set up a series of workshops devoted to the writing of short monologues along the theme of confession. Most of the pieces in the present volume were written during three workshops at the Arches Theatre in Glasgow between 2003 and 2005. The participants had different expertise which was a bonus. There were writers and aspiring writers, writer-performers, writer-actor-directors and actors. Walter Manfre and I conducted the first week's workshop, with the idea of following the format of the Italian *Confession*. The group, however, quickly made me understand that this would be impossible. In actual fact the thematic and stylistic diversity of these short plays reflects the participants' cultural, linguistic and religious heterogeneity. Glasgow is a truly multicultural city and while the majority of people attending the workshop hail from Scotland, others come from England, Ireland, Iran, Italy, Nigeria and Australia. Before writing began, our discussions pivoted on different concepts of 'confession', and thereby sin and guilt in contemporary society. Confession of one's sins to a Catholic priest proved significant for only a small portion of participants, who were of different faiths, agnostics and non-believers. For many, verbs like 'confide', 'unburden', 'co-opt' were more congenial than 'confess', as were alternative figures, such as counsellor, therapist, psychoanalyst or simply a friend, acquaintance, or passerby rather than a priest.

In later workshops I invited the group to explore a fraught situation, where the protagonist feels an overwhelming need to confess or simply to reveal something for the first time. As the plays developed, the performers in the group began acting them out, so that the writer and the rest of us could get a feel of the text in performance. It soon became clear what was working and what was not. This collaboration between author and performer proved vital to the process as did Andy Arnold's involvement. The experience and sensitivity of this director helped writers to take their work a step further and made them realise the potential of their play onstage.

In the end the plays amount to a form of theatrical storytelling which undermines our usual notions of what theatre and theatre-going mean; in performance a dynamic interpersonal interaction comes into being, where the actor repeats the same story for each audience member in turn, while the spectator becomes a kind of actor with a string of roles to perform as she or he listens as the actor unloads his or her guilt, reacts, and might ultimately become complicit with what is being revealed. In 2005 Andy Arnold's production in the atmospheric labyrinthine space of the Arches magically brought these plays to life.

I would like to thank the Scottish Arts Council for a development fund, Andy Arnold, artistic director at the Arches, who kindly hosted the workshops and directed the first production, Jean Cameron, then programmer at the Arches, who generously guided us in the early stages, and Louisa-Jane, arts administrator, who took over at a later stage. I'm also grateful to Andrew Dallmeyer, Ann Marie Di Mambro, Iain Heggie and Pauline Goldsmith who did not take part in the workshop but agreed to write for the project. Many thanks to Wilma G. Stark who believed in the concept from the word go, Hugh Hodgart at the Royal Scottish Acdemy of Music and Drama who supported the project and to his student actors and the professional actors (some of whom took part in the workshops) who performed the monologues.

Alan Cesarano produced a DVD of the show, details of which can be found on: www.alancesarano.com

Maggie Rose 2007

Production Note

Before *I Confess* I had not experienced one to one theatre. I had come close to it as a director with a recent production of *Beowulf* – a promenade piece with a large cast and where at certain moments members of the chorus would each grab hold of an individual audience member to make a particular plea. But these were brief flashes before audience and performers returned to the safety of their groups. With *I Confess* the performance itself was to one audience member alone and this gave it a totally different chemistry – new territory for me as a director and new territory for the actors and the audience. I have always believed in aiming to have the actors and the audience inhabit the same world and this one to one confrontation took the dynamic to its logical conclusion. Suddenly the audience member was an unsuspecting partner in a symbiotic relationship – a private witness to a terrible deed, the sole auditor of awful admissions. With some confessions the audience member watched a performer look away with little or no eye contact. With others, the audience member was directly addressed, with searching eyes, sometimes scoffed at or challenged, sometimes intimidated or shouted at. Without the safety of numbers or the anonymity of the seating bank, there was no escape.

The range of confessions varied a great deal. Some,

like Lynsey Murdoch's travel agent's account of landing her ex-boyfriend in a Bangkok jail, were darkly humorous. In others, like Aicia Devine's *When I was Six*, performed by a grown woman holding a doll, were both compelling and deeply disturbing. There were sex addicts, wife beaters, depressed mothers, people brutalised by their childhood memories, and so on. The list may appear grim. But the experience of listening to these confessions was strangely uplifting and liberating.

The task of staging these confessions was a challenging one – sometimes feeling like a military operation. Much of the rehearsal period involved my watching individual rehearsals with a stop watch in my hand – the running time of each being crucial to the mechanics of the whole production. One confession lasting twenty seconds too long along side another which was twenty seconds too short would result in a growing log jam in the flow of audience members from one story to the next.

Planning the audience journey around the basement spaces of the Arches was complex but we were blessed with the provision of a highly resourceful and atmospheric site specific performance space. There were in fact nineteen confessions and I worked out two routes of ten audience members on two separate circuits around corridors and hidden recesses. One performer, a deaf mute, performed Gerry Loose's story of an exasperated single mother in sign language to two audience members at a time – one from each group. Thus the two performance groups collided briefly at the border to watch this extraordinary signed performance before returning to their separate worlds.

The thing was that whatever confession you listened

to first – and each audience member started at a different place – at the end you felt you had gone on your own private journey – the cast had all performed to you and you alone.

Andy Arnold 2007

Crystal Anne

Lynsey Murdoch

CRYSTAL ANNE, mid to late twenties. Smartly dressed in travel agent's uniform with a name badge.

CRYSTAL ANNE: Hello, hello! Please come in, take a seat. Welcome to 'Distant Dreams' travel agency! Now, how can I help you? Are you looking for a holiday?

There's some great deals on for the independent traveller. Do you want me to set you up with something? Y'know we try and sell the customer the most expensive holiday; package it all up then add on a few 'service' fees for ourselves. That's business. But when I see a real traveller, like you, I do my best to get them the cheapest and easiest holiday possible – it's not even a holiday, it's an adventure.

I don't even add on as many service fees and for Robert (**beat**) I didn't add any at all. Robert was independent, no . . . he was free. He hadn't been long back from Africa when he came into the shop. Botswana, Zimbabwe, Maaadagascar! He looked . . . wow. Just *wow*. I did honestly think that Antonio Banderas has walked in, I did! Brown skin and dark hair – gorgeous dark eyes as well and when he spoke! I melted – that accent!

I wanted to touch him. As soon as I saw him I touched the skin that had sensed a new place.

I could see all the girls were dead jealous when he sat on *my* desk. He smelt of the sun and he gave me this huuuuge smile:

'Hey Crystal Anne, you look like you know what I'm looking for – got any good packages to Bangkok?'

'Bangkok!' I repeated and spouted off everything I knew about it. It impressed him. He began to ask me questions about Bangkok as if I'd been there.

So I told him I had. I pulled the images and all the sumptuous words from the pages of the *Rough Guide* and created a Bangkok so beautiful, so Far Away. It was so indulgent and spectacular . . . I don't blame him for asking me out that night.

We fell in love. Me with his stories and his freedom. He fell in love with my lies.

I researched Bangkok in the shop when I wasn't seeing Robert during the day. I looked up places I was going to say I had been to. For weeks that's all I would do, all day. My boss had to give me a written warning but I didn't care. I didn't care so much it was scary.

I was in love, with the travelling man. When I was with Robert I had been travelling. I was like him. Free, touched by the Far Away. I became interesting and *beautiful*. I was new. We would smoke hash in the living room of Stu, Rob's pal and laugh . . . I felt bad. It was great.

Robert and I were together for six weeks when he asked me to come with him. I was so excited I said yes straight away, but, the lie began to creep up and knock on my conscience's door. I had seen Bangkok in Robert's eyes. But I hadn't. Robert's eyes, were shining with the prospect of being taken around Bangkok by me; this was going to be his 'best adventure ever' he told me. I lived with the flurries of excitement and guilt for months. The whole shop was talking about it, 'I didn't know you'd been to Bangkok!' I was scared but then I was new, the lie had made me new. I didn't want to let it go now that I had finally found it.

So when Robert told me he didn't want me to go . . . When he told me I didn't fit into his plan . . .

'You asked me to go with you,' I told him.

'Things have changed babe,' he said, 'Travelling is my thing – it's something I do on my own.'

I argued. I screamed. I cried. I demanded he take me.

But he was going to leave me.

It took a few days to really sink in. I even took my 'Sights of Bangkok' wallpaper off my computer. I started working again. The boss said he was glad I had given up on my 'silly little pursuits'. He never liked 'indies' – they never spent enough money.

I arranged to meet Robert on the day he was due to leave. I told him all was forgiven.

'You're the best,' he said, 'A superstar – the coolest chica around,' and gave me one last wee kiss.

I wanted to give him something that would add to his experience, really make it his own. As he abandoned me on the grey shores, I wanted to know that he would remember me. So I went to Stu and I bought every ounce of hash he had. Everything. Pills and powder – whatever. He didn't want to sell me it, but the few thousand pounds I had saved up for going away swung him to give me it all. I took it all home and put it in an empty cake box, tied with a silver bow.

Robert told me that he would e-mail me. He said I belonged here, in my little job, in this little world. I told him not to open the cake until he got to his hostel in Bangkok. I made him promise.

He promised. Y'know he was worried about squashing it. I told him it would taste just as nice. Sweet.

Do you know what they do to travellers they find with drugs on them? It's awful . . .

Long pause.

Now, do you want me to see what packages I can offer *you*? Portugal? Alaska? I've always wanted to go to Alaska! (**Beat.**) We could go together! No, no . . . I'm kidding . . . we couldn't do that could we? (**She smiles hopefully at the customer**.) . . . No, no . . . (**Spots next customer waiting**.) Oh, well I'll let you think about it. (**To next customer.**) Yes, come in, come in! Sit down. (**To current customer**.) Remember, I'm always here! Bye now!

Not Yet

Alexander Hutchison

**M has just watched his mother die and describes her
final hours and the conflicting emotions he has experienced during that memorable day – including the
strange and disturbing twist at the end.**

M: I don't know what it was. Early afternoon. I must have
forgotten something. I just went back up to the flat for a
minute, and I was heading out the door again when the
phone went. But if I hadn't come in *just then* I wouldn't
have got it at all – not in time.

My sister Jean. I had to get back up home as soon as
I could. I said: 'That's sudden'. Don't know why I said that
– but I'd only been back in the city a couple of days
before.

God, four hours' drive! It was Easter time. Good
Friday. Can't really remember the weather – not too bad
– clear and cold. Got duller – *dreich* – the further North
I went.

Oh, and Jeezo – nearly forgot. I had just got into the
car – maybe two or three minutes along the road –

noticed the oil warning light was on! Christ. Pulled over – opened the bonnet – oil everywhere! Whoever put the oil cap on at the last service couldn't have done it properly – it had popped and everything was sprayed up inside.

Panic. Mercy. What'll I do? But there was a fancy car dealership right there – so I barged in to the showroom and told the story – said it had just happened – could I fill her up and risk it? They weren't sure – but why not? So we did – they must have had oil – and I was on the road again. It worked okay – but fraught! God.

There's a poem John Donne wrote about 'Good Friday . . . Riding Westward' – Don't suppose you know it? Seventeenth century. Aye, metaphysical. 'Burn off my rust and my deformity.' Spiritual crisis of some sort, most like. Well, he didn't have transport problems like I had: not first thing!

Still, four hours on the road gives you some time to get composed. Though no idea just what I would find. But I remember when I came down over the braes and got the first view of the sea – that first real pang – then it was only a few minutes to the door and straight in.

The sound was right there – straightaway. My sisters were there of course – and I must have greeted them – but the first words out of my mouth, hearing that sound, were: 'Is that my mother?'

I don't know if you've ever heard it yourself – and I don't know if I can describe it to you now – but it *tears* at you. And this was so loud. They call it a death-rattle – well maybe it is, but this one rasped and gasped and *sounded,* God knows: it filled the whole place. That was seven or half past. She didn't die till close to one. And it must have gone on since the morphine shot in the morning. No wonder Jean was a bit short on the phone.

What can you say when you watch your mother die – or *being dead and still dying.* That was more what it was like: there was no Mum left really – she was stretched out, propped up a bit – and the noise just kept coming out of her. Her face was so thin. Like an effigy. People say that – I know. But it was true. Waxy, bony, yellowy skin. And the noise. Not constant: she would pause. Not shift, just pause. Then it would cut in again.

I held her hand, sat in alongside. My sisters stayed through the house. Left us alone. I stayed with her for that last time. I remembered choo-chooing her through to the bathroom just the week before – me supporting her from behind and both of us laughing going down the hall. Choo-choo.

We had made up a lot of ground between us those weeks. A lot. You have to understand: she was a strong clear, pure will my mother. Brought up not to work – but the way things turned out she had to. Worked hard. Hard on herself: expecting a lot of others. Always a perfectionist. I've got it too. I try to relax – and chill – and *do* – but still feel like she did – *Properly: do it right if you are going to do it at all.*

Well there she was – past consciousness, past any awareness surely, but still rasping her life out as I sat by and held her hand.

Then a change in the pattern – the dreadful roar went

down (it *did* give you dread – like when it first hit me coming in the door) and now the breath starting to fade. I'd been talking on and off, but just said: 'There you go. We love you. That's you. We love you.' Eventually it stopped. Everything was quiet again in that wee room.

Well. What happened next is what this is about. All sound is gone. My mother's gone. She's stiff and stark. Her eyes are open – but nothing is there. I wait and wait a bit longer. I'm not quite sure. Eventually I reach over and with my thumb and forefinger brush down over her lids to close them. *Back they come on* – open wide – no sound, no movement – but these eyes didn't want to close – not someone else closing them anyway. Open – dead, but *not yet*. Can you imagine how that felt?

I never told anyone that till now. I didn't tell my sisters at the time – nor later.

The black framed notice was in the Registrar's window first thing next morning – caught poor old Lizzie out, her friend, just heading for the shops. She came to the door in tears.

But what about those eyes – persisting? Up to the very end.

Not till I say so. You don't need to do it. Not that way. Not yet.

Can You Hear Me?

Tom Murray

A woman, forty. Her home.

WOMAN: Can you hear me? In there. Inside me. The nurse at the hospital told me babies can hear. . . . Understand things while they're . . . She has to be right. She has to.

You have to be able to . . .

Winces.

. . . understand.

Please.

Winces.

I'll put on my teacher's voice.

Winces.

You have to lie still.

Can you hear your Mother's heartbeat? The most

natural sound in the world to a child in the womb, so they say. It's why we were given wombs. It's our role in life.

I am born. I give life. I die.

Can you hear your mother's heartbeat? No. For your mother doesn't have a heart. That's what they would say. Everybody. If they knew how she really felt.

If they knew her.

If they knew. . . . Me.

For she knows you're real now. No more sticking her head in the sand. No telling herself that forty year olds don't get pregnant. No more beating herself up for twenty years of being careful and then one bottle of wine too many.

She was almost there.

Your brother finally getting a place of his own. No more pretence. That's what she thought.

She was wrong.

For the camera never lies. **(She picks up a baby scan photo.)** That's you in the photograph. That's one of your legs. So the doctor said. Never could . . . Just one big blur. To your mother. Not real.

Winces.

But then I saw what the doctor saw.

Winces.

You have to lie still. Let me say what I have to . . . need to say. For you are real.

And soon enough the whole world will be *oooing* and *ahhhing* when you make your appearance. And you'll be going to nursery. And school. And not wanting away from your mother's side and looking at . . . her . . . me . . . for motherly . . .

But don't worry. For your mother will be there. She will. To wipe your nose. Pick you up when you fall. Give you . . . hugs.

Your mother will be there.

No choice.

She realised that a long time ago. Twenty years of playing Colin's perfect mother.

No . . .

No problem . . .

. . . to her . . . Body ripped . . . ripped . . . in two, stitches . . . itching, aching, tits . . . tits bursting with milk and some . . . some . . . some bloody . . . bloody, bloody helpful cheery bloody nurse.

(Nurses voice.) 'Just give it time.'

Hands. His little hands. Scratching at my breast . . . breasts . . . Little . . . His tiny little mouth . . . searching.

(Nurse's voice.) 'Just give it time.'

Finding.

Draining me dry and the . . .

(Nurse's voice.) 'There you go. You're a natural.'

Echoing down the bloody years.

Everybody. Twenty years of . . . everybody. My mother. Mother and toddlers. Nursery. School. Everybody.

Winces.

You have to lie still.

Winces.

Echoing. 'You're a natural.'

Well I'm not. Can you hear me? I'm not . . . I'm not a natural.

I'm not natural.

Don't you come into this world expecting motherly love.
Don't expect.

I can't. Back then I didn't understand. I only knew something was missing. Colin so tiny lying in my arms and everybody . . .

But not me.

Something missing. And I cried. Years of feeling guilty.

I felt nothing.

For that baby in my arms. Nothing. No bond. No motherly love. I didn't hate him, or feel resentful but I couldn't love your brother like a mother should. Like all the books tell you.

I never have.

Winces.

You can hear me.

Winces.

Please understand. Your mother is tired.

Winces.

Your mother is sorry. So sorry.

I can only offer you so much.

I can be your mother but can't be your mum.

Therapist

Stewart Ennis

He looks her in the eye. He is perfectly still and silent.

Slowly, with his eyes only, he looks her up and down, lingering on her breasts and her thighs . . .

He raises his eyebrows. He slowly winks at her. He licks his lips very slowly.

He half smiles. He is quiet, self contained, polite and charming.

MAN: Sorry. I was distracted.

He eyes her up and down again but doesn't linger this time.

So. Here we are.

He waits for reply. Of course there is none.

I see. Of course. It's going to be one of those sessions. Where I do all the talking. Very good.

Raises his eyebrows in anticipation of an answer.

Okay. Let's try this. (**Pause**.) You're a good looking woman.

He smiles.

Or am I not allowed to say that? OK. So what I'm think-ing . . . I mean, 'What's on top!' is this; you are a good looking woman. You have a nice face. Nice eyes. Nice mouth. You're wearing nice clothes.

He looks at her breasts.

You're a . . . nice woman. A nice . . . *person*. (**Pause**.) More?

He watches her chest.

I love the way your chest moves; up . . . and down.

He breathes slowly and deeply.

And you're clever. I like that. I do. I like intelligent women; intelligent . . . *people*.

He breathes in and out slowly and deeply

But most importantly . . .I *respec*t you. I find you attractive and intelligent . . . *and* I *respect* you.

He can't believe she is still not replying. Looks at her with mock suspicion.

I know this is cheeky. But do you speak *English*?
Aapko angrezi atii hai? Aapkaa naam kyaa hai?
Urdu. A language worth knowing these days. In Great Britain.
No? *Parlez-vous francais*?

Pause.

Don't worry.

Pause.

You're doing well you know. Keeping me talking. *That's* clever. Well, I suppose you *have* to be clever to be in a job like this. Mm? Is it the same training as a *doctor*? Five years at university, One *years* clinical experience etc . . . etc? Or, is it more like . . . counselling?

He nods.

I imagine it's more like counselling. You can do that over six weekends can't you? You find a lot of *women* doing counselling don't you. It used to be hairdressers.

He smiles.

Now its counsellors.

He leans in towards her.

Between you and me, and these four walls, I'd sooner come to you to have my hair done, than to be told how to run my family. But, you asked me to be here . . . and I was too polite to refuse. So, here I am.

Again he breathes deeply and slowly in and out.

I'm a *doctor*. I'm a good *doctor*. But if I don't sit here like a naughty school boy and acknowledge my domestic misdemeanours then you will take my stethoscope away . . . and not give it back.

So. Friends, Romans . . . etcetera.

He raises his hand, looks at it and quickly adjusts it . . . as if to take an oath.

I realise that slapping my wife's face is not the most efficient way of stopping her from provoking me.

He looks for response.

Okay? . . . Yes? . . . No? . . . What?

He looks for response.

Is it the content you don't like? Or the tone? . . . Or what? You're not going to tell me are you? Sorry. I forgot. I have to find it *within myself*. OK. How about this. Giving my wife a black eye will not prevent her from antagonizing me. Yes? No? Goodness me. This is trickier than I thought.

He rubs his chin in a theatrical fashion.

Thrashing *my wife* with *my belt* is not compatible with being a registered doctor; nor with being a respectable member of society. No? Why not?

He quickly takes off his belt.

Look, well within the Rule of Thumb.

He looks for response.

No? Oh *alright* then: I-must-not-hit-my-wife. It-is-a-bad-thing.

Smiles.

There we are. That wasn't too difficult was it?

As the woman he is talking to gets up to leave he calls out after her.

Short back and sides please love.

A Talking-Stick Confession

Skye Loneragan

MISHA, a woman in her early thirties, is cradling a bonsai, in an office, by a desk, reading the note that came with it. There is something deeply disturbing about the message.

MISHA: **(to bonsai)** If anyone cares for your welfare they should confiscate you. All plants die in my care. And it's not that I don't talk to them.

MISHA is pacing, nervous. Note in hand.

Oh, this is ridiculous.

She goes to make a phone call, stops.

He must have got out of jail. He must have – **(referring to the bonsai)** – maybe it's poisonous.

Oh, God, why didn't I open my mouth?

(Reading the note.) Call this number? Oh God, how can I. Tell them, what? . . .

Reacts to a sound . . . it's nothing.

(Hugs bonsai, whispers) . . . I can't believe he's found me. He's angry. I think he's angry. Jeb Fenton never got angry.

(To bonsai) You're not poisonous, are you?
This is ridiculous, Mish. Just do what it says, Mish, just . . .

(Goes to call) . . . I can't. I can't.
It's too late, Jeb! It's too late to open my mouth.

What could I say to the police after all this time? What are they going to do?

Curls up under the desk, foetal, taking the bonsai with her.

I should have stayed up there, tucked between those branches, a twelve-year-old runaway, waiting for some-one to notice.

At thirty-three, I'm still waiting for someone to notice. To miss the whole absence of me, to notice, oh, look, she's gone, that I've left the room. Do we ever grow up?

You were a lot bigger than me, Jeb. The police . . . I thought somehow they must know, we were friends. That you told me about the rings, in the tree trunk. Showed me the sap. That we sat together . . .

And yes, it was all, 'What's happened to your face?' and 'How did this happen?'

– because of the bruise, there was a bruise on my

face where I . . . I think I must have hit myself climbing up there . . . I was going to live up there, in the branches . . . I didn't even think of supplies . . . but you got me down in the morning, I'd never been to the police station . . . and they were asking me, because of the bruise.

They were asking *you*

'How did she get this?'

They wanted to know how it got there.

I could have just said. 'No, it wasn't you.'

Why didn't I just open my mouth?

I saw you everyday in that park. So I wanted you to –

I know, I know, I'm stubborn and it took you most of the morning to get me down.

You wouldn't leave me alone. Circling. You weren't giving up. You couldn't believe I got up so high.

You just sat there. You said you'd given me the talking stick, now why wasn't I using it?

It was a twig. Just a twig. Didn't help, ran home with it but they didn't notice I wasn't there.

But it was how it became that talking stick, that's what got me down off that limb.

You said, a young girl runs away from home, climbs a tree, dies of silence and becomes a branch. The tree adopts her and turns her soul into a branch . . . the weight of her silence bends the bough . . .

She breaks the branch of the bonsai.

(To bonsai) I'm sorry. I told you you wouldn't last. This is ridiculous, Mish, what are you doing curled up under your desk. **(Coming out from under desk.)** Such a surprised gulp in your eyes when I came out from under that table. I don't know how the police didn't see me there. Such a sad screwy face . . . when I asked you to adopt me.

Do we ever learn?

Adopt me and I'll tell them, I said. You wouldn't, you couldn't. You had kids of your own.

I know I asked you to hug me. I know you wouldn't. I know I told you that you could touch me there. But to me it meant, a gift . . . it was the only way I knew to . . . I know you didn't.

I know I wanted you to. I know they thought you did. I know I said nothing. I know I said nothing.

I know I wanted you to touch me.

This is ridiculous.

Comes out from under the desk.

I'm thirty-three now, I'm Jesus-dying age, and everytime I meet a man I want the same thing, the same thing I never – the knowledge that I am . . . that I'm . . . fuckable. Touchable. Nothing but sex on a stick. Nothing but a moving mirage of want.

I confess I wish I were the one. I wanted to be the one. The one that Dad wanted to touch. I wanted to be wanted. I wanted his big shoulders loving *me*. I wanted him to have chosen . . . me. Not her. Not them. Not the sister above me and then the one below me, and take long showers and . . .

Grow up, Mish, for God's sake. It's your birthday and you will just have to say sorry to this tree surgeon.

Goes to call again. Throws the phone. Childish tantrum.

Why, why did he go through two sisters first and never even look my way? Why did they get to go on holidays to places more than two hours away in a car with him, reading the map and stopping for ice-cream? Why did I have to wait in the dark hearing sounds that never came my way?

Oh I know. I know. I should be very, very glad. I love my sisters. It's not something anyone with any sense of decency would wish for. But everytime I come across big shoulders, everytime I meet a man, a man I could wrestle with, a man I want to touch . . . everytime it drips back into . . . this. This need. This ugly stretching absence. This thing I never got when I was too young to see. . . They would tell me desire is a disgusting thing from that angle, from that age.

MISHA is sinking down, against the wall.

And they're right.

And at thirty-three I've learnt . . . nothing.

It's not shifted. In all that time. I still want to be the one with the Vaseline.

No wonder I can't make this call.

No wonder I've already ruined your chances: **(Referring to the bonsai and the broken branch.)**

No wonder I am talking to a tree.

Nothing to Confess

Iain Heggie

No particular prop requirements. A man in his twenties.

Longish Pause.

MAN: Wasn't even my idea, coming.

Beat.

Ex-girlfriend actually.
Her suggestion.
Thought I'd give it a try.

Beat.

But I can't think of a single solitary thing . . .
'I have nothing to confess except I have nothing to confess.'

Beat.

I must of done something though.
Surely.

Well seemingly 'we are all sinners!'

Beat.

No.
Nothing yet.

Beat.

Always reckoned confession's a bit of a wank myself.
You know.
Fill up on sinning till you're ready to burst.
In you go to the wee booth.
Bit of quick relief.
Out you go.
Right as rain.

Beat.

Still can't think of anything.
I'll keep trying.

Beat.

Oh got one.
I killed my ex-girlfriend's new boyfriend!

Beat.

Not really.
You get that, right?
I was only joking.
Not violent-natured me.

Have to be driven to it.

Beat.

Mean: What if you're on a bus?
One time?
Bunch of scallies get on.
Walk straight past the driver.
Not paying.
The driver gets out her seat.
It's a wee woman.
She follows them.
They're sitting up the back
Refusing to pay up.
She's standing up to them all the same.
Staying calm.
Not taking any lip.
But there's a whole gang of them.
Firing insults at her.
Poking her from all sides.
It's getting a wee bit hairy.
Bus is packed.
But no one's looking round.
Everyone's like staring straight ahead.
Muttering about being in a hurry.
But no doing anything.
And your girlfriend's sitting there beside you.
And you want to show her you're not scared.

You can handle the situation.

That you'll get up and say something.

Put those scally boys in their place.

But then again.

You might make it worse.

The ex might be the one that gets it.

Off of the scallies.

And it'll be your fault.

So you do nothing.

Just wait and see what happens.

Then bit of luck.

Couple of cops turn up.

And get them off.

Beat.

Trying to work that one out.

Reach a conclusion.

Being cautious in a tricky situation.

Does *that* count as a confession?

Not that the ex has got any doubts.

Off the bus.

And all the way up the road

she's like nip nip nip

'You should have said something.

You're a grown man.

They were only wee boys.

The abuse that poor wee woman had to take.

If it had of been me would you have done the same?'

On and on she goes.

On and on and on.

She wouldn't shut up.

She just wouldn't shut up.

So I just . . .

Well it was her own fault.

If she'd had more comprehension

it wouldn't have happened.

Makes no difference though.

You still end up feeling in the wrong.

Hard to avoid feeling bad

When you hear your ex's jaw crack.

And she's lying there.

In the gutter.

Screaming.

Blood gushing out her conk.

Beat.

And actually my ex dumped me

over the head of it.

And she still hasn't given me one good reason!

So I was like:

OK, if I go to confession will you go back with me?

She's like:

I'm seeing someone else

So I'm like:

So what's the point of making me go?

So she's like:

Maybe you'll learn something

Beat.

Don't see how.

Between you and me.

Mean: what's the point in struggling with it?

Trying to make up sins out of thin air.

Confessing for confessing's sake.

I'll just have to accept it

I was right all along

I have nothing to confess.

Just Looking

Eliza Shackleton

Liz aged thirty-nine, attractive, intense and slightly bitter. She hasn't been lucky in love and is panicking about her biological clock ticking. She is in her new boyfriend's flat, nosing around and rifling through his belongings.

LIZ: Do you know something? I don't think you really ever get to know somebody until you've been to their house. How can you? If you've never seen someone in their own corner of the world, then you don't really know the *real* person do you?

I love going to someone's house. It's my favourite thing. I could spend all day in other people's houses, just looking at their bits and pieces. I just get a feeling about what they're really like. Not what they want to be, but what they are! I can tell everything I need to know just by looking at their things and how they arrange them. Don't say anything but, I have this irresistible desire to look through their drawers when they go to the toilet. Do you do that? Or is it just me? I bet you do! You look like the type! I'm just having a nose. I really try hard not to but, I just can't help myself.

I'm just looking! Not touching, not stealing. I just like to know what I'm dealing with!

Don't say anything for God's sake, cos I don't want this getting out but, whenever I'm seeing someone new and I've gone round to his house for the first time. Well, the first thing I do is to send him to the shop to get me some chocolate. When he's gone I think to myself; **(Looks at her watch.)** Right! I've got about five to ten minutes. Steady! Ready? Go! I go through his bag, drawers, have a good look round his bedroom, bedside cabinet (that's crucial by the way!) and his bank statements, of course! Anywhere secrets lie. I don't like to leave any stone unturned. And that's how it should be! After all if he's got nothing to hide, then what's the problem? It's all right for me to be mysterious. In fact, I think it's very attractive, so I've been told anyway. **(She flirts with the male audience member.)** But I don't like him being mysterious. It's just not allowed!

I won't wait you know! I can't wait! I will *not* wait weeks, months, years even! While he quietly reveals himself to me, bit by bit, telling me and showing me what he thinks I want to see. Glossing over things, being economical with the truth. I don't have the luxury of having time for that. If I don't have all the facts, all the nitty gritty, how can I make a decision *now?* I want to know this second when am I moving in? I need to pack. Where am I going to put all my stuff? I've got loads of things! I'll just have to pack some of his stuff away. **(Brings out a black plastic binliner.)** Actually, I'll just chuck it out it. Saves time.

Oh my God! That wallpaper is minging, it's got to go! When are we getting married? What date this month? It's all right I've ordered the dress, booked the church, I made the cake weeks ago. It's all under control, every angle has been covered. I'm not just a pretty face, you know!

This house is far too small and pokey for my liking. We will just have to move. I'll start looking today. Especially, when the children arrive.

(Looks at her watch.) I want babies now! By the way. Not tomorrow. Not next week. *Now!* They're bound to have his baby blue eyes. I'm not mad about green and I just don't do brown. What's next? I'm thinking house in the country, dog, Bob's a nice name, grandchildren . . .

(Looks at her watch.) I don't know if you've noticed? But I don't do any of this seeing each other business, you know, let's see how it goes kind of thing. I prefer the let's just get on with it approach. *Bring it on!* No! I can't have a meaningful relationship with a man whose bed I haven't looked under. Oh my God! What the hell am I thinking about? THE SHEETS! **(She rushes to the bed and sniffs the sheets.)** Not too bad! Smelt a lot worse! Let's face it if a man doesn't smell right it's just not going to work is it? It's the beginning of the end. **(She starts looking under the bed and spies a box full of photos and letters.)** Ah Hah! What's this! And as for pictures of old girlfriends? Bucket! He won't be needing these anymore; he's got me now!

Chucks photos, letters, etc in black bin-liner.

I have to do this you know, it's for his own good! Having a five-minute rake through his things tells me more about him than seeing him three times a week for a year ever could! Anyway if he really thinks that I'm not going to do that, well, he's obviously a bit of a daftie isn't he? I don't know about you but I'm not really interested in dafties.

Actress improvises certain comments according to the male audience member she is performing for. These comments are geared to make him feel slightly self-conscious and uncomfortable. Comments might include:

Do you blow-dry your hair? Oh! Control Freak! You obviously had a domineering mother!

Oh I can see you've dyed it as well! I don't know what I think about that! Oh! Pinkie ring, that say's it all, deceitfulness! Don't go there! Oh dear! Your shoes! Have you only got the one pair? That just says it all! I bet your house is a state!

(She looks at her watch.) Oh! Here he comes, God he was quick! I like that in a man! Mind you if I ever caught anyone snooping through my drawers I wouldn't be happy. In fact, I would call the police, because that's different. A girl's got to have a few secrets. **(To herself.)** Haven't we girls?

The Wedding Present

Mahmood Farzan

MAN: I had just got home. I made a cup of coffee and sat in front of the television. I was halfway through drinking it when the awful news broke.

I sat pinned to my seat. A submarine earthquake. Mountainous seas rising out of the depths and crashing onto the coasts, destroying everything. The sheer force of nature exposing the feebleness of man.

The taste of coffee in my mouth turned bitter, a bitterness which became more and more unbearable as the hours of news revealed the depth of the tragedy. The word 'Thailand', repeated with every news bulletin, tore my heart open.

I was desperate. Two days previously I had spoken to them. Ali and Jo had contacted me as soon as they'd landed in Bangkok to say how happy they were to have agreed to my suggestion. It was the last time I spoke to them, telling me they would be in touch again soon.

I knew Ali from Iran. Jo was Irish, very open and friendly. They had met here at University, and fallen in love. They were well-suited, kind and easy going. Ali was one of those friends you could always rely on – if he said he'd do something he'd do it. Jo too was very loyal and steady, although funny and always smiling. They had been living together for about two years and had decided to get married.

Well actually, it all started as a joke. One day, when I was round at their place I said, 'You two are so fond of each other, you get on so well, why aren't you getting married?'.

'Because we can't afford it'. Said Jo; then Ali said,

'Yeh, a wedding reception and a honeymoon in Spain . . . ', which made me say,

'Whenever we mention holidays or travel you immediately think of Europe, and especially Spain; there are so many wonderful countries in the world to visit.'

'Like where?' they asked. 'America? Australia? – yes but the tickets cost a fortune!'

'What about Asia or Africa?'

'Well, they're expensive to get to too,' said Jo.

'Yes, but once you get there it's very cheap as long as you choose the right place,' I said.

'So where?'

'Look, I'll pay for the tickets as long as you agree to go

where I suggest and you can judge if it was a good choice when you get back'.

Then Ali said, 'But why should you pay?'

'It would be my wedding present to you. . . .'

Ali looked at Jo. 'Well Barley, what do you think?'

You see, sometimes Ali used to call her 'Barley' because 'Jo' in Persian means barley. She would always laugh and say if I'm Barley, then you must be Alley Lane!

Although she'd been several times, Jo was keen on Spain, she hadn't even thought about Africa or Asia, but in the end she was persuaded.

'Yes, it would be good to go somewhere different for a honeymoon.'

And I said, 'Thailand . . . I'll pay for the tickets and you can pay for the rest. It's very cheap and your normal spending here will be more than adequate, so it won't cost you.'

' . . . Alright then', said Jo, and when I suggested that Christmas and New Year was a romantic time to honeymoon they happily gave in and we set the date. Believe me, no one can feel the bitter sweet of that happiness as I do.

It was three months till Christmas, plenty of time for Ali and Jo to organize the wedding and arrange the reception, and I made myself as helpful as possible. Now I can only wish that I had never suggested the idea, or that they had never accepted it. I don't know if perhaps this was to be their fate and they couldn't have avoided what happened – but I really loved them and I wanted to help them.

Sometimes I wonder if the horror of the sunami makes my memories of them even more vivid, more precious. Then I torment myself with the thought that I sent them there, but then who sent all the other thousands who died, miles to the north, south, east and west? We are tied to our destiny, a destiny that we make for ourselves with our own actions.

Alley and Barley never came back but their memory will live in my heart. They are in a land where earthquakes will not reach them and where they will grow, mature and bear fruit.

Erotomanica

Pauline Goldsmith

Erotomanica – To be in love with someone you have never actually met. And you know they feel the same. It's a recognized disorder, but we've all been there – haven't we? Based on a soap opera friend of mine who is constantly attracting the kindness of strangers.

Stunned to meet the object of his/her affections B (audience member), A is nervous, euphoric and shy.

A catches sight of B.

A is stunned when he/she sees B.

Looks away at first, then steals glances until gradually A is staring at B.

A: How are you doing?

You're looking great!

I love your hair.

You really suit your hair like that.

It's lovely, so it is.

I really like it like that – I liked it curly too but that really suits you as well.

I didn't like it when you had it all kinda . . . **(Wiggles hands round the aura of his/her own head.)** Remember? So so how are you? You look great.

I thought it was you. I recognised your hands. Honestly, as soon as I saw your hands, I knew it was you!

Isn't that funny?

Pause.

You're looking much better. I was so worried about you! You handled that all brilliantly I tell you.

I don't know how you did it. I said a prayer for ya – I did. I lit a wee candle for you too. No, I did!

That's gorgeous that top – it's lovely. Is that the one you had on that day at the hospital? It's lovely – you always suited that colour.

Pause.

God. **(Internal laugh.)**

I can't believe I saw your hands.

Pause.

Margaret said she'd seen you. And d'you know I *knew* I was going to bump into ya today. Like I knew. Honestly. I swear to God. Isn't that weird?

Pause.

Did you get my card? I tried to send you a birthday card but I think it was an old address.

Honestly, I didn't forget. No. I swear – I'd never forget an Aquarian's – Capricorn maybe, but not yours!

I sent you an invite in it to blow out wee Sarah's candles but you mustn't have got it.

God. **(Internal laugh.)**

Takes in the beautiful scenery of B's face. Longer pause.

Anyway . . . it's been lovely to see you.

You take care of yourself. Be good to yourself. Okay

A leans in to kiss B goodbye but lingers in anticipation of a more loving kiss. A pulls back abruptly as he/she realises the intimacy is not complicit.

Sorry, I totally misread that. Sorry. Sorry.

Wait – please –

Sorry, can I . . . can I say this?

I don't want to freak you out. But – I've got to say this.

God, look at me.

I'm always like this with you.

It's like . . . I don't . . . then there you are and suddenly I can feel my whole body alive.

Sorry I don't mean in a rude way but it's like meeting the other magnet. I *feel* . . .

I can feel it in my throat – It must be my shakras opening or something.

No, seriously, I'm . . . God . . . I love you.

I love you.

What ever that means. **(Laughs.)**

God, it's all coming out dead clichéd but I it's like . . . I just feel this electricity – and I think . . . bite the bullet

. . . I think you are a beautiful, incredible, amazing individual

And no matter what happens –

You keep me going.

You are the reason I get out of bed in the morning.

I swam an extra length for you today.

You know . . . I think what you've been through and it keeps me going. I just think you're . . . **(Laughs.)** Sorry.

A rummages around taking out a pen and a piece of paper and gives it to B.

Anyway, I'll not keep you. I know you're still with Viv and . . . that's really cool.

Could you make it out 'with love to Jennifer.' Cheers. Thanks.

As B autographs the paper or refuses the autograph, A takes out mobile phone or disposable camera and puts one arm round B and takes photo with other hand. Waits for the flash light then presses the button.

Okay, one two three . . . Love You!

Hooked on High

Mary Wells

Character is Maxine Kolbe, from Dublin, in her twenties. Post-argument mascara damage on her cheeks. Shifty air of desperation, yet still exudes equanimous charm.

MAXINE: Hello Father! Me again.

I know, I know I just got absolution, but . . . look – I sinned on the way out. I was wondering if you do a dose of the strong stuff this time? Grand!

She sits, and says, bowing her head.

So God help me Father for I have sinned and stuff.

Pause.
She looks up.

That's it now!

She bows her head.
Pause.
She looks up.

That's it with the hands now.

She bows her head.
Pause.
She looks up.

What's the matter? You're looking at me as if I am some sort of tool.

Oh – the sin! Haha, well, I walked out of here and I thought . . . I thought a terrible thought, Father.

Her eyes dart and linger on his hands.

I thought 'I really want to hurt somebody'.

She searches his face.

With a knife? . . .

I want to hurt a child?

You know, the little ones with their shining eyes and unconditional love and trust. I get them to huff on turps and feed them to pit bulls!

. . . I am thinking of becoming a protestant?

What kind of a priest are you? Get the hands on for Christ's sake!

Pause.

Oh fuck – I just blasphemed at you. I am so sorry.

Look Father, you don't really want some sort of inner wound do you? I mean, come on, I don't have any dark secrets to confess! I'm lucky, I've had a happy life, you know? There's nothing wrong with it at all – middle class, privileged, all of that.

She breaks into racking sobs.

But I just feel so guilty about it!

And snaps back.

That's about the best I can do.

A hand. A thumb. A pinkie? I don't know why you're playing so hard to get. You're as bad as Sean. Yes, Sean's back. Oh I don't mean he went anywhere, I just only see his back these days. It's not very good between us. He doesn't understand all of this – not like you. You're *ordained*.

I can only imagine what that felt like. A sort of long mellow buzz. . . . Or a speedy rush, like a communion? Hey, I'll tell you something for nothing though – have you ever had the last rites? See when you're knocking about with those fellas from St Mathilda's – oh yeah, putting away the last of the sacrament wine, making an incense bong out a baptism bath and a coupla hymn books – get one of those auld fellas to lay on the hands and do that. It's wild! I had it by mistake and it was the bollix. The hands were on, and that was *it*. I sat up, poker straight – you know like in films when they've had a bad dream – and all of this pestilence and thick black smoke comes roaring out of my mouth, on and on and on like a flood, as loud as a waterfall, and all of these bluebottles fall out of my arse. Anyway, as soon as it arrived it's gone again; just a little wisp coming out of my ears.

Me and the priest, a lovely bloke from – now where was he from? That's it, Liverpool – are just sort of staring at each other. And then, it kicks in. This *feeling*. Sheer, pure *joy* – and I was *flooded* with it.

And it lasted. A coupla months actually. And if I am honest it's never been quite the same since . . . it's different. Rapturous. Ecstatic. Peaceful. But never so sort of complete. Now I think every time I am blessed now it's getting quicker, y'know, the feeling doesn't last past a coupla minutes now . . . Father.

She pointedly eyes his hands.

These shooting pains up my arms are getting worse though I tell you. Ow, Oh, Oh my g –

She clasps her chest and keels over athletically, with a gurgle of agony that you would expect from something Greek. Long pause. Sheepishly she dusts off and sits again.

Some Christian you are.

Come on, what are we supposed to do here? Oh, you are so in cahoots with Sean! Trying to turkey me into stopping. Well, you have to want to stop and I don't. I can't. What is so wrong with wanting to be happy? You know what? – Ask anyone. Ask anyone in their deepest, most private moment, 'are you truly happy?' Well one per cent will say 'yes'. So of course I'm a fecking addict, I don't want to join the ranks of the miserable like everyone else. Oh it's alright for you, you can bless yourself whever you want, but I'm supposed to go home now! I'm supposed to go home and go back to being normal, just like that. Well you know what? You know what? Leave me alone.

She leaves.

A pause.

She returns.

Please don't leave me alone.
No! You know what? Leave me alone!

She leaves.

A pause.

She returns.

Please don't leave me alone.
Get off! Leave me alone!

She leaves.

A pause.

She returns.

Please don't. **(She is teary, and full sobs come.)** Please don't leave me alone.

A pause.

I'm sorry about that Father.

She gathers herself together. She sneezes.

Don't! Say it.
I'd better start somewhere.

Oh come on, Father, wish me luck.

She extends her hand for his handshake. She retracts hers, quickly.

Actually – Better not shake on it just yet.

She leaves.

The River

Lynsey Murdoch

MARCUS is in his mid-thirties to early forties. He wears a winter coat and chitters throughout with the cold. He does not make eye contact at first. Then he looks. There is a moment of quiet shock and he looks away again and struggles to begin speaking.

Eventually . . .

MARCUS: I've been looking for you for a wee while.

It's hard to . . . It's hard to look at you.

Pause, he slowly looks up.

You're older.

I thought, well, I thought you'd be a wee girl and I could just . . . y'know . . . give you some story about heaven and . . .

Looking away.

I'm sorry . . . I'm so sorry. **(Beat.)** I didn't know.

Pause.

I take a walk everyday at the river – it helps me. Rivers change, all the time. Always renewing. Washing your sins away.

Everyday I go and see this yacht there. It's moored on the left bank – it's fine. Huge. White. Beautiful. I look at her and I imagine . . . **(He imagines.)** The main deck, me taking the wheel as a warm wind blows her along and I sail, sail, sail her away into the blue and violet evening sky. It's a stupid daydream but it just keeps me going.

That's where I was, in my dream, on the main deck when I . . . It's dead quiet down there, especially at this time of year. I can be alone for hours so when I saw your Dad . . . **(Quietly.)** I'll no pretend ah didn't get a fright.

He was a bit further up stream and I didn't know what he was, at first. I thought he was . . . I don't know. It was dusk y'see. All I could see was this black shape, like a . . . like a stone.

For a second ah couldnae move and then I realised . . .

It was a man, just.

In a suit. No much older than me. His tie was waving in the wind – bright red. I remember that.

He was just a few feet away.

Staring he wis, at the water.

No dreaming like I was, just staring.

Pause.

I knew. Oh I knew.

I've been there.

At the side of that river, wantin it, urging it to swallow me up.

There was peace then, in the mucky depths.

I don't know how long he stood there, how long I sat and watched.

Cos suddenly he crouched down – almost fell.

The sun went down. How quickly it gets dark.

He pulled off his tie. And let it go, it flew by me – like a wee red bird. It disappeared into the sky. **(Softly.)** Free.

I looked back at your Dad . . .

He was trying to . . . struggling **(Beat.)** to get in.

I could just see his face, and then, just the top of his hair, then his hand, one hand, clinging on – knuckles white.

I thought for a second he didnae want to do it, y'know that part of yea that clings on to life and I got up. I stood up . . .

But he let go.

Pause.

He just looked lost. He looked already dead. I . . . I . . . **(Beat.)** I could see . . . his eyes when he wis floating there – no tears.

His suit was dissolving in the brown water, y'know like tissue paper. Just ebbing away. Water was edging up over his arms.

I could only make out his face. The silence. Oh, the silence. No a sound.

Creeping, just creeping bit by bit the river swallowed his

face. Then just the tip of his nose. Still breathing . . . still holding on? I don't know . . .

Cos then there was nothing.

I understood. I understood him perfectly.

I didn't want to stop him.

I let him die.

Pause.

Then I saw you. Where your Dad had been.

I watched you twirling on the surface like a waterlily. You danced towards the riverside and I . . . I picked you up.

A small, crumpled photograph of a little girl.

I didn't know.

I though he had nothing, like I did. I know what that's like when there is nothing, nothing that is no touched with soulless darkness and . . . and . . .

Pause.

He'd been holding you in his hand.

Monk

Andrew Dallmeyer

A chair with a stool beside it The audience member sits on the chair. Enter the monk. He kneels on the floor, leaning forward on the stool.

MONK: Confessor, I confess.

I confess to you, Confessor.

I confess to you my manifold sins. Firstly I have committed the sin of gluttony. At supper time the day before yesterday I took two slices of ginger cake where one would have sufficed. Much of my day dreaming is taken up with visions of pies and pastries with their yellow and brown crusted roofs and the succulent meats that lie beneath, steaming with heat and dripping with juices. I dream of quivering chunks of poultry peeled from the bone, slippery fruits, gorgeous green peas with butter and mint. Pepper and pineapple. Sugar and cinnamon. But above all I dream of roast potatoes, hard and crisp in their dark brown armour but with soft white centres that crumble and melt. Sometimes I salivate for minutes on end like one of Pavlov's poor dogs!

And drinks. I dream of drinks. Fine red wines from Bordeaux and Burgandy. Rich ruby Rioja matured in oak casks. The pear and apple flavours of Chablis and Sancerre. Brandy and Champagne. Sherry and Armagnac. The very names enough to ravish the senses. Medoc and Beaujolais and Chateauneuf du Pape.

I confess to this and seek absolution.

Secondly I have committed the sin of sloth. On this very morning, when the bell sounded in the belfry and we were summoned to prayers, I lingered late and lay longer than was necessary. And as I lazed and dozed, unclean thoughts came crowding unbidden into my fevered mind. And here must confront another sin, which Is the dreadful sin of lust.

Many hours I spend dreaming of the soft flesh of women, of caressing their rounded breasts with their tender cherry-stone tips. I imagine my hand along the swell of their hips, the gentle curve of their belly with its tuft of fuzz. I long to savour the delicate juices of their excitement and touch their moistening crevices that lie at the very fork of this wiliowy and scented species. Such imagery leads me inevitably to arousal and sometimes I relieve myself in the vile practice of self-abuse! I confess to this sin. **(He rises from kneeling and sits.)**

But above all, my greatest sin is the sin of anger and wrath. I confess to overwhelming feelings of rage. I rant and rage against all inequality. Against all systems of authority. Leaders, Rulers, Kings and Queens. Politicians with their lies and lust for power. Those who know what's best for others. And block free passage of their brothers. No more imposition from above! Avoiding Power is True

Love. So here's an end to special people with charmed existence, magic lives. Princes, Monarchs, Saints and Stars, It's all designed to keep you small. To keep you down and in your place. But the rules of life are the same for us all. Everybody gets a similar ration ot boredom, irritation and depression. Everybody sits on the lavatory. Everybody gets old and dies. No special lives! No special people! No superiors or judges! No imposition of one will upon another. **(Now standing.)** Who dares now sit in judgement? By what authority is he so high and mighty? No more people like yourself. No more Father Confessors. Who are you to hear my confession? You will doubtless reply that you have God's authority, but God will surely know no hierarchy. You sit, you listen and you presume to know. You offer guidance. How can this be so? You are no more than I. No better. You too have been greedy, slothtul and filled with lust. Admit that my graphic descriptions excited you, my lustful words ignited you. Such is the hypocrisy ot power. And yet you set yourself as being beyond reproach and this is why I now confess to the sin ot anger and rage. Because of you! And people like you! You are the cause of my distress. Now get down on your knees and confess to me! **(He points to the ground.)** Confess to me, Confessor! Confess to me! On bended knee!

Venus

Wilma G. Stark

Venus McGregor, twenty-eight, disabled since birth; in a wheelchair. She can get out, with a struggle, and the help of two sticks, if required; Catholic; never had sex; goes to confessional; no access into booth so has to have confessional directly with 'Priest?'; confesses to always thinking about sex; however not pathetic; not melodramatic; she is feisty; has attitude; kicks ass!

Follows others into confessionals. Head down – rosary in hand.

VENUS: Bless me Father.

It's been too long since my last confession.

Looks up.

Are you a priest? A *real* priest? **(Touches his knee.)**

How old are you?

I'm twenty-eight, you know . . . and I can't stop thinking about . . .

I've never . . . really . . .

Head down.

I've never been . . . Oh God, I might as well say it . . .
(Head up.) *Shagged*!

I keep saying it! And I keep wanting it! I just want to go up to guys in pubs these days, and say, 'I suppose a shag's out the question?' or 'Any chance of a shag?'

Aw, don't be like them and just think . . . 'She's a poor wee cripple. I'll just tell her to say ten Hail Mary's and a Glory Be, . . . Peace be with you, my child' . . . and send me on my way!

Glory? Glorious? It's not in the least glorious, I've had no Glory. . . . At least not in the sense of *two* bodies becoming *one*!

Are you just like everybody else, thinking 'cause my legs and arms don't work, then neither does my brain, or my hormones for that matter; so I'll not think of sex and I'll not *need* it or *want* it?

Head down.

Lord have mercy!

Head up.

Is that so terrible? So bad?

Keep busy, my counsellor says – just keep yourself busy. God does she think – same as all you probably – that I just sit with my bum super-glued to this big meccano set **(Touches chair.)** and look out the window or watch television? And that everybody else farts around about me, doing everything for me? Huh, if that was the case, how could I not get one of those 'Farters' to *shag* me now and again? Eh? Or is that not for *folk like me*?

Head down.

Christ . . . have . . . mercy . . .

I don't see why not?

Head up.

Everywhere you look, nowadays, *sex* is on display. It's on the TV – old people, young people, men, women, even all those nature programmes –

Birds, bees, lions, tigers . . . *turtles*. All the pop songs are about *it* . . . the adverts . . . films . . . there's just sex, sex, sex everywhere – on the streets, on the buses, and trains, planes, and the internet!

Well, I see these things too. And do you know something? *I'm jealous*! I'm screaming inside – 'oh God, I wish that was *me*!' *I . . . really . . . wish . . . that . . .was . . . me!*

Does that make me bad? Drowning in Sin?

Thats me up to *twenty* 'Hail Mary's' now? Or maybe more? Oh, and you better throw in a dozen 'Glory Be's'!
(Raises arms with difficulty.) *Lord . . . have . . . mercy.*

Head down. Starts to cross herself.

Father, Son, and . . . **(stops)** *. . . Holy Mary, Mother of God . . .*

Head up.

Huh! Yes . . . *Holy* Mary . . . *Virgin* Mary.

Oh God, I'd say 'Hail Mary's' and 'Glory Be's' non-stop for a week, just to be able to say 'I've done *it*' . . . been shagged. . . . fucked. . . . Oh just to feel somebody up inside me . . . somebo . . .

Head down, shakes it.

Oh Christ . . . **(makes sign of cross)** *Have* . . . *Mercy.*
Keep busy? Keep busy?

Head up.

Look . . . I keep busy. I work, you know. Monday to Friday. Nine to five. I never have any spare time. These wheels of mine – they are red hot! Always spinning, here, there and everywhere. I've had a go at everything. Snowboarding; hand-gliding; even canoed up the Amazon! But I've never *shagged! Never been shagged!*

Shakes her head again.

Been there, *nearly* done it! Huh! Even had a moment of reaching the greatest heights, haha, and the earth definitely moved! But it was just ten thousand feet up a mountain in the Italian Dolomites, in the middle of an earthquake!

Pause.

But oh! That's not enough. I want more! I *need* more. I want to experience human contact . . . skin to skin . . . a warm body pressed next to mine . . . a real physical union . . .

Nearly made it . . . gave this guy a run home one night, from the pub, hah! On my wheelchair! He sat on my knees and we 'wheeched' up Great Western Road. He had his hand inside my jacket, right up inside my jumper; it was warm against my ti . . . Oh it was great. He was absolutely piss*ed, drunk* and the stupid bastard forgot to mention he lived up three flights of stairs! So we tried *it* on the bottom stairs. But he passed out just when I thought I was going to have it at last! Ach, I covered up his dignity, and left him there, on the bottom stair, and 'wheech'd' on my way . . . *solo* . . . *as usual*!

I was screaming inside! I'm still screaming! – but sometimes not just *inside*!

Pause.

I used to dream about . . . *making love* . . . but now I don't care . . . a *shag*'ll do . . . it's the best I can hope for!

Head down, shaking it in despair.

Oh . . . Christ . . . have . . . mercy!

Pause. head up.

Em . . . *are* you a priest? . . . a *real* priest?
If not? . . .
I suppose a *shag's* out the question?

Head down.

Oh, I know, I know. . . . Peace be with you . . . and also with *you*!

She struggles to rise.

Peace? Huh? . . . If only . . .

The Self Confessed Male

Martin O'Connor

One

MAN: All these things go through my mind. I confess. I'm sorry if it makes you uncomfortable.

I'm not here to criticize you. I'm not trying to reclaim anything.

I have to give you the best sex ever.

Would you want to mate with me? No?

So what is my penance? Secrecy. I have to keep this to myself. And even if I don't tell anyone will I be forgiven?

Two

MAN: All these things go through my mind. I confess. I'm a man. I'm sorry if it makes you uncomfortable. But I'm not sorry for who I am.

I'm not seeking anything. I'm not here to criticize you. I'm not trying to reclaim anything.

I have to give you the best sex ever.

Would you want to mate with me? No?

So what is my penance? Secrecy. I have to keep this to myself or else I will be labelled. And even if I don't tell anyone will I be forgiven for harbouring these thoughts?

Three

MAN: All these things go through my mind every time that happens. I confess. I'm a man. I'm sorry if it makes you uncomfortable. But I'm not sorry for who I am.

I'm not seeking anything. Anything other than the right to exist. To survive. I'm not here to criticize you. I applaud you. I'm not trying to reclaim anything like the right to scratch my balls or leave the toilet seat up, or any of those clichés you find in magazines.

Magazines that declare I have to give you the best sex ever – even though I have no chance because I can't locate the several G-Spots.

Magazines that proclaim a smoother body is preferable – that hair is unsightly. Would you want to mate with me? No?

So what is my penance? Secrecy. I have to keep this to myself or else I will be labelled a misogynist. Or a chauvinist. Or a sexist. Then I'll have my penis lobbed off which would prove extremely fitting, seeing as I'm only ruled by what is between my legs. And even if I don't tell anyone will I be forgiven for harbouring these wicked, un-pure thoughts?

Four

MAN: All these things go through my mind every time that happens. Every time, my gender is to blame. I confess. I'm a man. I'm sorry if it makes you uncomfortable. But I'm not sorry for who I am. I admit it. I'm a man.

I'm not seeking anything. Anything other than the right to exist. To survive. I'm not here to criticize you or your movement. I applaud you. I'm not trying to reclaim anything like the right to scratch my balls or leave the toilet seat up, or any of those clichés you find in magazines.

Magazines that declare I have to give you the best sex ever – even though I have no chance because I can't locate the several G-Spots hidden throughout your body because I missed last week's issue.

Magazines that proclaim a smoother body is preferable – that hair is unsightly. Would you want to mate with me? No! Because I have hair on my arse and shoulders. So due to natural selection, women are eradicating the hairy gene.

So what is my penance? Secrecy. I have to keep this to myself or else I will be labelled a misogynist. Or a chauvinist. Or a sexist. Then I'll have my penis lobbed off which would prove extremely fitting, seeing as I'm only ruled by what is between my legs, then it'll be thrown out by the side of the road like that guy in America. And even if I don't tell anyone will I be forgiven for harbouring these wicked, un-pure thoughts? For to speak the unspeakable is to incur wrath.

Five

MAN: All these things go through my mind every time that happens. Every time you say 'You're such a man,' and every time my gender is to blame. I confess. I'm a man. I'm sorry if it makes you uncomfortable. But I'm not sorry for who I am. I admit it. I'm a man.

I'm not seeking anything. Anything other than the right to exist. To survive. I'm not here to criticize you or your movement. I applaud you. I only want the same. I'm not trying to reclaim anything like the right to scratch my balls or leave the toilet seat up, or any of those clichés you find in magazines.

Magazines that declare I have to give you the best sex ever – even though I have no chance because I can't locate the several G-Spots hidden throughout your body because I missed last weeks issue which also included 'One Hundred and One Ways to Pleasure Her During Her Period' – and don't get me started on 'Top Ten Tips To Titillate Her Tiny Treasure'.

Magazines that proclaim a smoother body is preferable – that hair is unsightly. Would you want to mate with me? No! Because I have hair on my arse and shoulders. So due to natural selection, women are eradicating the hairy gene, forcing us to be more like you in mind and body.

So what is my penance? Secrecy. I have to keep this to myself or else I will be labelled a misogynist. Or a chauvinist. Or a sexist. Then you'll hunt me down and I'll have my penis lobbed off which would prove extremely fitting, seeing as I'm only ruled by what is between my legs, then it'll be thrown out by the side of the road like that guy in America but that's okay he got what was coming he deserved it and anyway it's nothing compared to the years *we've* had to suffer because of men like him. And even if I don't tell anyone, will I be forgiven for harbouring these wicked, un-pure thoughts? For to speak the unspeakable is to incur wrath. Your wrath. But that's okay. Because your feelings count.

When I was Six

Alicia Devine

**A young woman is sitting with a large doll on her
knee. She is about sixteen or seventeen years old
with an air of distractedness about her; she seems
like an overgrown child. She looks unkempt and
neglected and appears anxious. She speaks with a
Scottish Western Isles accent.**

YOUNG WOMAN: Do you like dolls?

Do men *have* dolls?

    I like dolls. I like it when their eyes close . . . like this
. . . then they're asleep. My favourite doll is Susan here.
I've had her for ages. Since I was six. Look at her. She's
big. Like me. She's the only person I play with. I don't
have any one else. I washed her hair last week and I put
conditioner and gel on it. Dipididoo. I think I can still
smell it on my hands.

She pauses and looks up nervously.

Have you come to take me to Glasgow?

Uncle Jamie brought me Susan from Glasgow. No shop on the island sells dolls as pretty as Susan.

Do you know the islands?

I like the beaches best. In the winter the waves sound like a washing machine . . . sh . . . sh . . . blots out the crying . . . you know . . . the gulls.

In the memory of this she seems to regress to her childhood. She speaks to the doll in her six year old voice.

I want to be a gull. I want to swoop down and catch a fish, or land on the water and float. But Uncle Jamie says people sink when they land in the water, if they can't swim, but if the waves are too high and the current's too strong it can carry you off.

She is back in the present. She has a thought.

You'll not carry me off will you? I've promised to tell you. My mum said if I didn't they'd take me away and lock me up **(as if in her mothers voice)** *'Like* they did to Jamie.'

This thought frightens her.

He stopped coming you see, when I was six. Six. My mum, she changed after he'd gone. She'd mutter under her breath over and over, 'Oh Jamie, Oh Jamie'. He was my favourite uncle better than Uncle William or Uncle Gordon, my dad's brothers.

Pause.

He held me tight. All over. I remember. I do remember

this . . . *honest*. He'd . . . he'd **(she hesitates, trying to find the right word)** . . . *tickle* me. I felt funny. Once I saw a girl kissing her boyfriend, I felt sort of tingly, like I wanted to go to the loo. Well I felt that way with Uncle Jamie, when he tickled me.

It never felt bad. Honest.

She looks up.

Are you a doctor?

My mum said you were a type of doctor? But you couldn't be cos you're not wearing a white coat. All doctors wear white coats don't they?

She is a young girl again. She addresses her doll.

He says I 'm his special girl and he'll love me forever and ever.

He says it's our secret and we don't need to tell mummy. I love having secrets.

Pause.

We play 'Secret' games with the Bible. You put your hand on it and swear things. Like this.

She puts out her hand to demonstrate.

'Mhairi, promise never to tell mummy that your Uncle Jamie loves you the best.'

'Promise'

'Promise never to tell mummy that Uncle Jamie gives you sweets,'

'Promise'

'Promise to never tell mummy that Uncle Jamie tickles you.'

With solemnity.

'Promise'

I love having secrets.

I'm Uncle Jamie's special girl like Susan is mine. I love being special.

Long pause. Her tone changes. She is back in the present.

Then one day he came to the house with a strange lady. He put his arm around her. Mummy was happy and kissed them both. He didn't even look at me. He didn't play with me or give me sweets and . . . and . . . I didn't feel tingly any more. I wanted him to tickle me.

Beat.

So I told mummy all our secrets. Everything . . . even . . . even if . . . I know it's bad to lie and I know it's bad to break a promise but he'd broken his. Why did I have to stop being special? My mum cried and cried and cried in the kitchen. She looked at me so queerly, like she hated me, 'You!' she said, 'Get up to your room and pray for God's mercy and don't come down until I tell you!'

This is her most painful memory. Pause.

Later I heard voices and shouting and then I saw Uncle Jamie leave with Mr McLeod. I watched them from the upstairs window till the police car disappeared over the hill. I never saw him again.

She looks up. She is anxious.

Is that okay then? You won't take me away now will you? Please don't take me away. My mum needs me. Uncle Jamie didn't mind. Honest. He even wrote and told me. I got a letter from him. He said I was a good girl and he meant no harm to me. He said he knew he'd never done anything against me and that he forgave me. He understood. Doesn't that make it all okay? My mum will love me now won't she? She'll be happy now I've told you, won't she?

With more awareness.

Some folk say I'm funny . . . you know . . . peculiar. Do you think so? Am I?

She disappears into her childhood safety once more.

This is Susan . . . she's my best friend. We play at houses on the beach. We listen to the gulls.

Biographies

ANDREW DALLMEYER has written sixty-five plays, won three Fringe Firsts and a BAFTA (Scotland) for the best radio play of 1985. He has directed some fifty productions in various repertory theatres. As an actor Andrew has appeared in every theatre in Scotland, with the exception of Pitlochry. His recent performances in Beckett's *Waiting for Godot* and *Krapp's Last Tape* (Arches, Glasgow) have been widely acclaimed.

ALICIA DEVINE has worked as an actor in the UK and abroad. TV and Film credits include Ken Loach's *Carla's Song* and BBC TV's *Get Carman* as well as appearances on ITV's *Rebus* and *Trial and Retribution*. Theatre includes: *The Well of the Saints* and *The Borrowers*. Her writing debut occurred at the 2003 Edinburgh Fringe, when her play, *Burns Night* achieved considerable acclaim.

STEWART ENNIS, actor, writer, teacher and photographer. Writing includes *The Darkroom, Robert Burns' Celtic Complex, Noah: Parts 1&2, Red Lorry Yellow* (via the Playwrights' Scotland IGNITE initiative) Also writing *Darwin's Tortoise* and some poems for *The Story Garden* project. Stewart was a founder member of Bench Tours Theatre and has worked with a number of Scottish theatre companies.

MAHMOOD FARZAN, was born in Iran. He moved to Britain in 2000 and reads and writes poetry. Since moving to Glasgow he has been involved in theatre and has started to write plays.'

PAULINE GOLDSMITH is an actress and performer from Belfast based in Glasgow. She has worked extensively in Scottish theatre. She was awarded The Stage Best Actress for Beckett's *Not I* in 2004 and a Creative Scotland Award in 2006. She toured her own Irish funeral show *Bright Colours Only* from Belfast to Brazil in a hearse.

IAIN HEGGIE was born in Glasgow in 1953 and started writing when he was thirty. He has written many plays including *A Wholly Healthy Glasgow* and *Wiping My Mother's Arse*. He has also adapted a number of plays and stories for theatre including *King Of Scotland* based on Gogol's *Diary Of A Madman*. He is a regular teacher of acting and improvisation. Currently he is Applied Humanities Research fellow in adaptation at the RSAMD in Glasgow.

ALEXANDER HUTCHISON was born and brought up in a fishing town on the north-east coast of Scotland. He has worked on and off in universities, including eighteen years in Canada and the USA. As a poet he has been published widely. His first collection, *Deep-Tap Tree* (University of Massachusetts Press, 1978), is still in print. *Scales Dog*, a gathering of new and selected work, was published by Salt Publishing, Cambridge in 2007.

SKYE LONERAGAN trained as an actor at Theatre Nepean, Sydney, and RSAMD, Glasgow. She wrote and performed *Cracked*, which won an Edinburgh Fringe First in 2001, toured internationally, and was commissioned as a radio play by ABC Radio National. Her other solo work includes *Unsex Me Here* and *My Right Thumb*. Her ensemble work includes *A Little Laugh I Lost Somewhere*, for The Arches Theatre, Young Directors Awards. She is currently Playwright in Residence with Visible Fictions Theatre Company.

LYNSEY MURDOCH has played such diverse roles as the First Witch in *Macbeth*, Benjamin in *Animal Farm* and *Pinocchio*! TV works includes a featured role as Maggie in ITV's *Taggart* and the award winning advert *Bland is Banned* for XFM Scotland. Her writing debut was the one woman show, *How to Eat?* performed by Lynsey at the Arches Live Festival in 2004. She has carried on her work with The Arches Theatre, writing a piece for the production, *Spend A Penny*.

TOM MURRAY is a full time writer living in the Scottish Borders. He is currently co-writer in Residence to Clackmannanshire Council. He is an editor of the literary magazine *The Eildon Tree,* and co-organised the 2005 Borders Book Festival fringe. His plays for both adults and young people have been performed at various venues including the Traverse Theatre, Edinburgh, and the Arches Theatre, Glasgow. In 2005 he was the winner of the Fish One Page Short Story Competition.

MARTIN O'CONNOR is an actor and writer. He has performed with The Citizens Theatre Company, Det Aapne Teater, Oslo, and TAG. He has written and performed three solo shows, *Manifesto, Zugzwang* and *Reality* for Arches Live, Arches Theatre Festival and Glasgay. Martin is also a co-producer of *Licence Pending*, a new Glasgow-based spoken word event.

ELIZA SHACKLETON is a graduate of the Arden School of Theatre, Manchester, and the Slade School of Fine Art, London. Her writing debut was with the one woman show, *Home Sweet Home*, performed at the Zion Theatre, Manchester, in 2004. She is a drama teacher and regularly exhibits her paintings.

WILMA G. STARK Writer and translator. Co-writer with Maggie Rose and Carlo Iacucci *Scars of War*, Edinburgh Fringe 2002; writer for *Travel and Tales*, Summerlee Heritage Museum 2005, North Lanarkshire Council; Translator of *Mad Cow*, produced by Arches Live 2005, written and directed by Alessandro Valenzisi. First full-length piece *Clara* written in collaboration with actor David Walshe, and with developmental support from Playwrights' Studio, Scotland, is now ready for production.

MARY WELLS trained as an actress at the RSAMD. Work since then has embraced a balance of classic and experimental and devised work: *King Lear* with Tag theatre, Viola in *Twelfth Night* and *Macbeth* with The Voice Studio, *Semi Detached* and *A Kind of Alaska,* Chichester Festival Theatre, *Faith Healer* and *Judith*, the Citizens Theatre and *The Woman who Cooked her Husband*. She has just performed in *Cyprus* for Mull Theatre, and is currently on a residency with Honolulu theatre in Hawaii.